DISCLAIMER OF LIABILITIES

WARNING:

The pictures, descriptions and procedures in this book have been developed with the safety of the horse owner foremost in mind. However, the dispositions of animals are unpredictable and varied and the Author assumes no liability, express or implied, for injury or death to any person or animal resulting from shoeing horses while following the instructions in this book.

Hooftrimming for Horseowners

by
David A. Duquette

3rd Edition, Copyright ©1996
David A. Duquette, Ed. S.

Cover Photo by Robert R. Lieske

ISBN Number 0-945782-02-0

Published by
H. F. H. Publications
P.O. 300
Lenoxdale, MA 01242
1-800-247-6551

 Printed on recycled paper with soybean oil based ink.

TABLE OF CONTENTS

INTRODUCTION

Why a book on hoof trimming written for the average horse owner? While I was a practicing farrier, many customers asked what hoof care they could do on their own horses, especially when a farrier was not available. In response to these inquiries, hoof care workshops were offered through local community colleges. These workshops demonstrated to horse owners the proper techniques and procedures for trimming and shoeing their horses. As the demand for the workshops grew, I found myself spending more time teaching hoof care throughout the United States and less time as a farrier. It became evident that a book to go with the workshops was needed. After searching for an appropriate book to use, I discovered that the books published were not written for the beginner or average horse owner. The books were written for professional farriers or for farrier education courses. While these books were adequate for that audience, they were not appropriate for the average concerned horse owner looking for information to help them.

In the course of teaching the workshops, through trial and error, specific techniques and basic methods were developed to simplify the steps in daily hoof care, hoof handling and hoof trimming. These techniques enable beginners to provide basic hoof care for their horses. This book as well as its companion book, *Horseshoeing for Horseowners*, is the result of 14 years of teaching horse owners how to work with their horses. These two books are the only books written by a certified farrier/educator based on a successful teaching method developed while actually teaching horse owners how to trim and shoe their horses.

Hooftrimming for Horseowners is intended for horse owners who are interested in learning why, how and when to trim. There are many things that can be done by an owner depending on the owners' motivation, talent, desire and ability. The information in this book will guide the horse owner with step by step instructions to: learn the necessary skills to pull shoes and trim hooves, gain confidence, improve existing skills and evaluate a professional farrier's work. This book is not intended to teach someone how to become a farrier. That is a long and continuing process that should only be done in an accredited farrier school. This book is intended to teach basic hoof care to horseowners to use with their own horses.

TOOLS

There are many horseshoeing tools a professional farrier needs but which a horse owner would find unnecessary. This section will only cover the tools needed for trimming or pulling old shoes. The author believes that only good quality tools should be purchased. This will be more expensive in the beginning but the tools will not wear out or break and good tools will make hoof care easier and allow the horse owner to do the best job possible.

Hoof Nipper - (cost around $50.00) Hoof nippers are used to trim the excess hoof wall. This is the most important tool needed by a horse owner that is going to work on their horse. Without a good quality hoof nipper it will be almost impossible for a beginner to cut the excess hoof wall level enough for a shoeing. Nippers come in 12", 13", 14" and 15" sizes. These sizes are the measurement of the length of the handles. The 15" nipper is recommended, as experience with teaching horse owners has shown that this size gives enough leverage, as well as accuracy, for the average saddle horse and owner.

Hoof nippers also come in various head styles. The only style to consider for the use intended in this book is the flat design. Other basic styles available (which should not be used) are: the overlap style where the cutting edge slides under one branch and the pointed edge where the branches meet but have a bevel on both sides similar to an axe or hatchet blade. It is extremely hard (if not impossible) to get a good level cut with these types of nippers. Since the quality of the trimming or shoeing job depends on the quality of the nippering job, the horse owner should get the best nippers available.

Hoof Knife - (cost around $10.00) The hoof knife is used to cut away dead sole from the bottom of the hoof, trim parts of the frog for hygienic reasons and to remove foreign materials from the foot.

Knives come in narrow and wide blade styles with the blade about 2 1/2 to 3" long. Hoof knives come in left-handed and right-handed styles, so be sure to purchase the right one for you. There is also a double sharp edge blade style.

Fig 1. Hoof Nipper - note the flat cutting edge.

Fig 2. Hoof Knives - (bottom knife right handed wide blade, top is a left handed narrow blade

The most common hoof knife in use, and the one recommended, is the wide blade single edge. The double edge knife is not really practical since much of the work done with the hoof knife is done with one thumb pushing on the back of the blade (with a double edge knife this can be uncomfortable!!). The wide blade is generally used since it will last longer when being sharpened as there is more blade to begin with. Most farriers would have a couple of knives, a wide blade for everyday hoof paring and a thin blade for hard-to-get corners, exploring abscesses, etc. The horse owner will only need one knife to do the work required. The knife should always be kept sharp and this is best accomplished with a round fine-cut file (rat tail file). This type of file can be purchased where chain saws are sold or a hardware store.

Horseshoeing Rasp - (cost around $10-$20) The rasp is used to level the bearing surface of the hoof wall after the excess wall of the foot has been removed with the nippers. The rasp is used to remove abnormal flares from the hoof. The rasp can also be used to remove burrs under the nail before clinching and to smooth the clinches during nailing shoes.

The most popular rasp is the 14" double extra-thin tanged rasp. This is a rasp with a coarse side for rapid hoof removal and a fine side for rasping the quarters during trimming and finishing the hoof. The fine side should be used most of the time. This will help limit the common mistake of rasping too much hoof wall when trimming and leaving a hoof low in spots. The rasp should have a wooden handle for safety.

Clinch Cutter - (cost around $8.00) The clinch cutter is used to remove the clinches when pulling old shoes off. A typical clinch cutter has two ends, the blade and the point. The blade is approximately 1" wide and is used to slide under the nail clinches and to cut or raise them when hit with the shoeing hammer. The point can be used to clean out the hoof instead of a hoof pick (see figure 35, page 29) The point can also be used to raise a nail head from the shoe crease sufficiently to allow it to be pulled out with nail nippers or pull offs when removing shoes. When purchasing a clinch cutter look for one that is flat on one side of the blade and has a slight bevel on the other side of the blade. This will make it easier to slide the clinch cutter blade under the clinch. The flat side of the blade is placed along side the hoof and the beveled side is placed under the nail clinch. Clinch cutters also work better if the blade is a little dull. This helps prevent cutting the hoof wall when lifting the clinches.

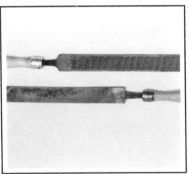

Fig 3. Horseshoeing Rasp - notice the fine and rough sides

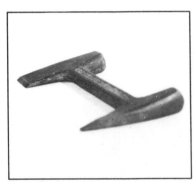

Fig 4. Clinch cutters

Shoe Pull Offs - (cost around $15.00) Pull offs are used to remove old shoes by sliding the jaws between the shoe and the hoof. Sometimes old hoof nippers can be used for this purpose if the blades are dull.

Shoeing Hammer - (cost around $20.00) Also called driving hammers, shoeing hammers are used to drive nails into the hoof, strike the clinch cutter when removing shoes and bend nails over after being driven through the hoof. Hammers come in several weights (10 oz, 14 oz, and 16 oz). The 14 oz or 10 oz sizes are recommended.

When choosing a driving hammer, look for one in which the striking face is as large as possible since this will facilitate driving nails for beginners. A light carpenter's hammer, no heavier than 16 oz, will work if necessary. Keep in mind that it is always better to have a hammer a little light than one that is heavy. If the hammer is too heavy, the horse might be sensitive to the pounding and the soft shoeing nails will tend to bend and warp as they are being driven into the hoof. Shoeing hammers also come with wooden and fiberglass handles. Either one will give adequate service.

Fig 5. Two different styles of shoe pull offs

Fig 6. 14oz. driving hammer

Shoeing Apron - (cost around $25.00) The shoeing apron is worn to protect the legs from nails during the shoeing process and the hoof wall edges during hoof handling. Although not absolutely necessary, it is recommended that one be purchased if you plan on doing much work with your horses. A hay apron may be substituted if the legging is long enough to cover the knee area on your legs. Additional protection you might wish to have is a pair of leather gloves (cost around $8.00). The gloves help protect your hands from rough and sharp hoof wall edges as well as nails and nail clinches.

Foot Stand - The foot stand is used to place the horse's foot on when clinching nails, finishing the foot or any other time the top of the foot is worked on. This tool is not absolutely necessary, as the foot can be brought forward on the horse owners's lap or leg. However, the author wants to strongly recommend—repeat strongly recommend—that everyone use a foot stand at all times the foot is brought forward. Most horses adjust to a foot stand rapidly even if not exposed to it before. The foot stand does take weight and strain off the horse owner's body and makes the job of working on the horse easier and safe. Stands can be fancy works of art or as simple as the agitator cone from a broken washing machine.

Fig 7. Shoeing apron and leather gloves

Fig 8. Foot stand made from disc harrow

The stand needs a center piece approximately 16-18" high and 2" in diameter. This center pole should be mounted on a wide base to give some support and to prevent the stand from being pushed over from the weight of the horse. The easiest kind of foot stand to make and also one of the most stable is one made out of an old disc from a disc harrow.

The tools needed to trim a horse are the hoof nippers, hoof knife, foot stand and a rasp. The tools needed to pull old shoes are the clinch cutter, shoe pull offs and driving hammer.

The trimming tools should cost approximately $70 to $80 (without the foot stand). A foot stand should be able to be made at a local welding shop for $5 to $10 labor plus parts. The tools used to pull shoes should cost approximately $30 to $40.

NOTES

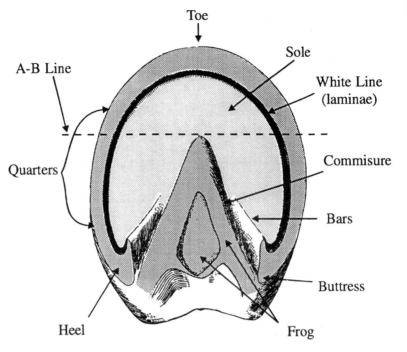

Diagram 1 - Hoof, bottom view

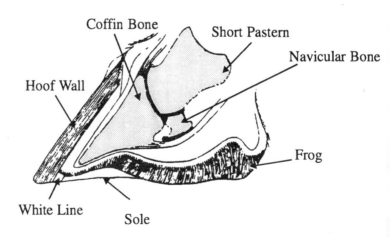

Diagram 2 - Hoof, cross section

ANATOMY

Every person that will work on their horse's hooves must have at least a basic understanding of the anatomy (structure) and physiology (function) of the horse's lower leg and hoof. There are many excellent books on anatomy that can be found in any library or book store. Therefore, the material presented in this section on anatomy is limited to the basic knowledge and principles that a person needs to know in order to understand what is involved in trimming. Please read this section while referring to the diagrams accompanying the text as necessary.

Shoeing a horse, at best, is a necessary evil. When more of the horse's hoof wall is worn off than the normal growth of the wall can replace, the horse needs shoes. Shoeing a horse's hoof can be harmful in several ways: 1) driving nails into the hoof causes damage in itself as well as leaving subsequent holes; 2) the unnatural elongation of the hoof wall by the shoe; 3) the added weight of the shoe; 4) can limit the expansion ability of the foot; and 5) lifts the hoof and frog off the ground which can limit their function. The author feels that because of these reasons that whenever possible, the horse should be allowed to go barefoot. This book will allow the reader to remove shoes when they are not necessary and trim the hoof properly to prevent damage. The following pages will help the horse owner understand the workings of the foot and how to trim the hoof based on the anatomy and physiology of the foot.

Structure - The hoof is made up of six main structures.

The *hoof wall* is the outside covering of the hoof. It is the part seen when the horse is in a standing position. The hoof wall varies in thickness from heel to toe. On an average saddle horse, the thickness of the hoof wall at the toe is approximately 1/2" thick while the thickness of the hoof wall in the area of the quarters is about half that. The wall is thickest at the toe where the wear is the greatest. As the horse picks his foot up to move, the toe is subjected to wear as the foot breaks over. The reduction in thickness at the quarters allows the wall to be flexible and expand with pressure. This helps absorb the tremendous concussion of the foot striking the ground.

The *periople* is the varnish-like covering of the hoof wall that helps protect the hoof while helping seal in moisture.

The *sole* covers the ground surface of the foot and protects the sensitive structures inside. The sole is concave in relation to the ground. The hind foot is generally more concave. This structure helps provide traction and non-slip function as the foot strikes the ground (similar to a suction cup). The sole is usually 3/8" thick where it unites with the white line and somewhat thinner toward the point of the frog. When a horse is barefoot, the sole will tend to flake or wear off naturally. When a horse has shoes on, the sole material can build up. Because of this, when a horse has been barefoot, less, if any, sole will need to be pared away than if the horse has had shoes on.

The *frog* is the triangle shaped projection located between the heels. The frog helps dissipate concussion (along with the foot expansion) and has a non-slipping function to help stabilize the foot. The frog is also elastic. It helps circulate blood up the horse's leg by compressing the plantar cushion (located above the frog) which is full of blood. The frog must be left large enough so that when the foot strikes the ground, the frog will make contact with the ground in order for the frog to accomplish these functions.

The *bars* are extensions of the hoof wall that extend from the buttress of the heel and parallel the side of the frog. The resulting groove or elongated depression formed between the bars and side of the frog is called the commissure.

The *white line* is the outer portion of the laminae system. The laminae are a series of interlocking tissues that unite and hold the outer hoof wall to the inner structures of the foot. The white line is made up of these interlocking laminae, the ends of which can be seen as the white line. It is usually not white but actually more of a pale yellow color and is about 1/8" in width.

The foot contains two bones and half of another. The coffin bone is extremely porous and is the bone that gives the outer hoof its shape. The porosity of the coffin bone allows it to be well supplied with nerves and permits tendons, ligaments, and collateral cartilages a strong attachment. The navicular bone is located at the junction of the coffin and short pastern bones. It provides a surface for the deep flexor tendon to slide over when flexing the foot. Although not a part of the foot, the long pastern bone is important in this discussion. The angle formed by the long and short pastern bones is the angle used when deciding at what angle to trim the hoof. (Refer to Diagram 4, page 35.)

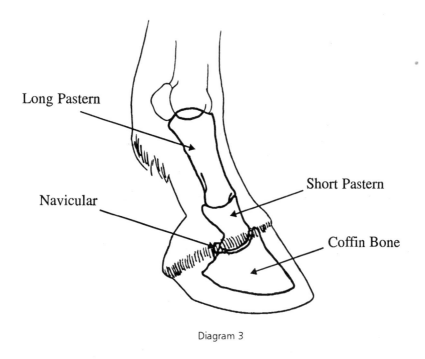

Long Pastern

Navicular

Short Pastern

Coffin Bone

Diagram 3

Function and effect on trimming and shoeing

The horse's foot is a complex, highly efficient structure. It provides supporting, anti-concussion, circulatory and non-slipping functions. The foot is made up of bones, ligaments, tendons, elastic structures, blood vessels and nerves.

The weight of the horse is supported by the bones, ligaments and tendons of the foot and leg. The weight is supported and transferred from the hoof to the body through the various bones, ligaments and tendons. As weight is applied to the leg, several things happen to absorb the concussion. The bones slide over each other slightly. The pastern sinks and the hoof expands. The frog makes contact with the ground and pushes up on the plantar cushion which then spreads the lateral cartilages. The heels expand with contact with the ground. Simultaneously, the blood in the various venous plexus (plantar cushion, lateral cartilages, etc.) forms a "hydraulic cushion," while the elasticity of the white line, sole and wall also help spread the shock throughout the entire foot.

It is important to allow the frog to have contact with the ground when trimming. If the frog is kept from making contact with the ground, (cutting off too much when trimming or excessive heel caulks on shoes), the plantar cushion will sink downward when the foot makes contact instead of being forced to expand upward by the frog. If this occurs, the lateral cartilages will be pulled inward and the hoof will contract instead of expand. This will prevent the foot from performing its major function of shock absorption and could cause lameness or injury to the horse.

The heels of the foot should not be prevented from expanding when the foot makes contact with the ground. This can be caused by excessive cutting of the heels in trimming, by nails being driven too far back in the foot or through improper fitting or shaping of the shoe. If the heels can not expand the plantar cushion and lateral cartilages will not expand as they should, thereby reducing the absorbing function of each.

NOTES

HORSE HANDLING

The assumption being made in this section is that the horse being worked with is gentle and has been shod many times before. If the horse is young, fractious or otherwise will not stand for shoeing, it is recommended that the horse owner seek professional help. It is hard enough to do a good shoeing job when the horse will cooperate and nearly impossible when the horse will not.

The area where the horse will be handled must be free of all debris and objects which could "spook" or injure the horse. The area should be one with which the horse is familiar and away from other activities which could distract the horse. The ideal area should be level, dry, protected from the elements, and with plenty of room in which to move around.

Whenever possible the horse should be held by a helper or a friend. Many horses will be easier to work with when a person is holding it. A holder can help control a horse that is acting up, nervous or other wise not standing for the hoof work. If the horse does act up, the holder can lead the horse's head toward the person working on the hoof. This will force the body of the horse away and minimize the chance of injury. Besides, companionship will also help the horse owner in another way—misery loves company.

When it is not possible to have a helper hold the horse, it must be tied. A strong halter and tie rope is a must. The halter should fit the horse properly, that is, not be too tight or too loose. In addition, the

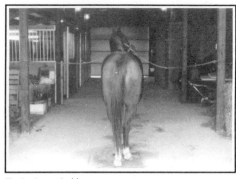

Fig 9. Cross tied horse

halter should be made out of nylon or similar material and be free of frayed or loose material. The rope used to tie the horse should be at least one inch thick and made of cotton. Tie the horse to a strong immoveable object with a halter and rope that will not break. Nothing is worse than a horse that has successfully broken free in the past. If a horse gets the notion that it can break free, nothing will be able to hold it.

The ideal way to tie a horse is to cross tie. Cross tying is done with the horse tied between two solid posts. From each post a rope is tied to either side of the halter. This method of tying is safest for both the horse owner and horse while working.

NOTES

HOOF HANDLING

Hoof handling is the hard part of shoeing or trimming the horse. If the horse owner can learn how to make the horse comfortable while working on the hoof, the job will be much easier for both the horse and horse owner. Most beginners will tire easily and forget to keep the proper positions for hoof handling. It is better to have the horse owner somewhat physically uncomfortable than to have the horse act up. If the horse is not comfortable it may act up, pull its foot away or lean on the person holding the foot. All of these actions will make it harder to do a good job. The horse owner should practice the positions and develop the muscles necessary (especially the thigh muscles) to get along with the horse rather than expect the horse to get along with a tired horse owner. If the horse owner gets tired or cramped, he should put the horse's foot down and rest. The horse will be easier to work with and hence make the job of shoeing and trimming easier for the horse owner.

Front Foot

Step 1   Slowly approach the horse from the head. Touch the horse on the upper neck near the mane. Rub and/or pat the horse. This not only establishes contact with the horse, but also lets it know you are there and gives you a clue as to how the horse might react to you.

Step 2   Facing the rear of the horse slide the hand near the horse down the leg from the shoulder. Stop in the middle of the cannon bone and squeeze the horse between the flexor tendon and bone. Squeezing here causes the leg muscle to relax as a reflex. At the same time pick up the foot with the other hand. You may need to lean into the horse's shoulder to cause it to shift its weight at the same time to the other front leg.

Fig 10. Establish contact with the horse

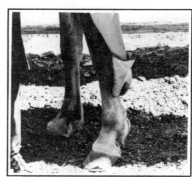
Fig 11. Squeeze the space between the flexon tendon and the cannon bone

Fig 12. Fold the leg up with the off hand

Fig 13. Change hands holding the foot

Fig 14. This is called the "home" position

Fig 15. Slide foot between your legs

Step 3   Immediately fold the leg up from the knee.

Step 4   Change hands holding the foot. That is change the foot from the hand away from the horse to the hand that is closer to the horse. This is called the "home" position.

Step 5   Slide the foot between your legs by passing the horse's leg through and between your legs.

Step 6   Position the foot slightly above your knees. Be sure enough foot is sticking out so you can work on it with your tools. (The foot will be held by your legs, slightly above the knee area. The area of the horse's leg that will be in contact with your leg is the pastern area above the foot.)

Fig 16. Position foot slightly above your knees

Fig 17. Be sure enough of foot is sticking out

Step 7   Turn your toes in and heels out while crouching slightly at the knee. Try to keep your back straight and bend at the knees. If you remember to point your toes and bend at the knees, the horse's leg will be firmly held. It is very important to keep yourself turned slightly into the horse. The horse's front leg is limited in its mobility (to the side) at the shoulder and knee. The shoulder and knee joint do not allow much movement to the side. What will happen as you get tired is that, unconsciously, your body will begin to drift out. This puts pressure on the horse's shoulder joint and the horse will begin to act up, not out of meanness but out of pain. Keep good position and the horse will tend to cooperate.

Front Foot Forward

The front foot must be brought forward (to the front of the horse) to shape the foot and to remove flares. Holding the foot in your lap in the forward position can be extremely dangerous and awkward. The horse can put its entire weight on you or your leg and there is nothing to prevent injury to yourself. For this reason a foot stand should always be used. The danger is minimized by having the horse's weight on the stand and not your legs.

Step 1   Place the foot stand in front of the horse.

Step 2   Go through the steps to get the foot in the home position as described in the previous section.

Step 3   As you turn to face the front of the horse and the foot stand, bring the foot forward and place it on the foot stand. The stand may need to be moved from side-to-side or forward-to-backward to allow the horse to be comfortable.

Fig 18. Place foot in home position.

Fig 19. Bring foot forward

Fig 20. Place foot on stand

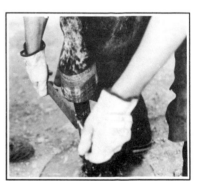
Fig 21. Stand to outside and behind foot

Step 4   Stand to the outside of the horse's leg and slightly behind. This will keep you out of the way if the horse takes its foot away or the foot falls off the stand. One foot may need to be placed on the base of the foot stand to help stabilize and keep it from tipping over.

Rear Foot

Step 1   Approach the horse from the front. Pat the horse on the neck to let it know you are there. Slide the hand near the horse along the back of the horse to its hip.

Step 2   Slide the hand down the back of the horse's leg to the middle of the cannon bone—midway between the hock and fetlock.

Fig 22. Slide near hand down the back to the hip

Fig 23. Slide hand to middle of cannon bone

Step 3   Lean slightly into the horse with your body and raise the leg toward you with the near hand. Always remain close to the horse. Your back should be in contact with the horse's side. This will keep you away from the danger of the horse kicking or striking out at you. By remaining close, the horse at best can only push you with its leg, not kick.

Step 4   Bring the hand away from the horse to the foot and grasp the toe, folding it up into itself.

Fig 24. Raise the leg and grasp the toe

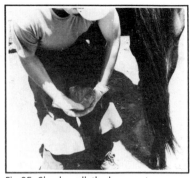

Fig 25. Slowly walk the horse out

Fig 26. The horse's leg should rest across your hip

Fig 27. Home position

Step 5   Step towards the rear of the horse with your leg that is furthest away from the horse. Bring your leg that is closest to the horse under the horse's leg at the cannon bone.

Step 6   Slowly "walk" the horse's leg out until you feel the horse relax. This "walk" should be accomplished by taking small steps. This will allow the horse to gradually relax its leg and hip muscles and prevent cramping or sudden jerks.

Step 7   The horse's leg should rest across your thigh with the foot resting on your outside knee. The area of the horse's leg around the hock will fit under your arm. This will give you more control in holding the leg and keep it from slipping. Point your toes inward, spread your heels and crouch. Let your legs do the work. This is the basic position for trimming the hoof. Some horses will be more comfortable stretched out behind while others will be more comfortable up close. You should be able to tell when the horse is comfortable as the horse will relax the leg muscles.

Home Position

With the horse's foot in your lap, grasp the toe with the near hand and step back into the horse—your back against the side of your horse. This is the "home position." This is a good position to return to any time the horse acts up while you are in the basic position. In this position you have some control and leverage over the horse and are out of harm's way.

NOTES

Bringing Rear Foot Forward

Step 1   Place foot stand under the horse.

Step 2   Place the rear foot into the home position as described previously.

Step 3   Bring the foot forward by grasping the leg in the middle of the cannon bone as you turn to face the front of the horse.

Step 4   Place the foot on the foot stand.

Fig 28. Place foot stand under the horse

Fig 29. Place foot in home position

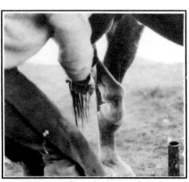
Fig 30. Turn to face the front of the horse

Fig 31. Bring foot forward

Step 5   Adjust the position of the stand according to the horse's comfort.

Step 6   Take your position to the rear and outside of the horse's foot.

Fig 32. Place foot on stand

Fig 33. Take position to the rear and outside of foot

NOTES

CLEANING THE FOOT

Anytime any work is to be done on the hoof, it must be cleaned. Wet mud can be cleaned off with a towel or cloth. Dry mud or dirt can be scraped off with the end of the rasp. Once the outside of the foot is cleaned, the foot can be picked up following the same steps that are used in the preceding section on hoof handling. By following the same steps and positions in picking up the foot for cleaning as in trimming the hoof, you will be training not only the horse but also your own body. The bottom of the foot can be cleaned with either a hoof pick, the back side of the hoof knife or the pointed side of the clinch cutter.

Step 1   Insert the pick (or other tool) into the compacted material at the rear of the commissure (between the frog and buttress of the heel) and push the pick through to the toe.

Step 2   Repeat this procedure on the other commissure.

Step 3   Pull the pick around the toe inside the shoe or hoof wall.

Proper cleaning of the foot is an important hygienic procedure and should be done anytime the horse owner is doing anything with the horse. Not only will it prevent most hoof disease but the owner can check for any foreign objects which could cause lameness. Regular cleaning of the foot also will help train the horse to stand for future shoeing and will help condition the horse owner also.

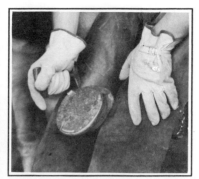

Fig 34. Put foot in shoeing position

Fig 35. Insert pick in one commissure - push to the toe

Fig 36. Insert pick in other commissure

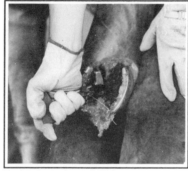

Fig 37. Push through to toe

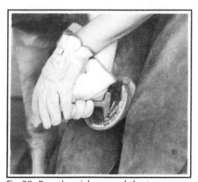

Fig 38. Run the pick around the toe

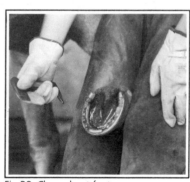

Fig 39. Cleaned out foot

TRIMMING — BAREFOOT

Trimming the horse's foot to go barefoot is the one thing that almost all horse owners can accomplish with a little practice. With regular and proper trimming, most horses with sound and healthy hooves can be used sensibly without having shoes on.

Trimming to go barefoot is done differently than when trimming to prepare the foot for a shoe. Generally the difference is in the amount of excess hoof wall cut off and the rounding of the edge of the hoof wall. When leaving a horse barefoot, more hoof wall (approximately 1/8" more) needs to be left projecting towards the ground surface. Think of the longer hoof wall acting as a shoe. The sharp edge of the hoof wall will also need to be well rounded with the rasp. This rounding will help prevent chipping of the hoof. Again think of this rounding as providing a natural 'shoe' on the barefoot hoof. When a horse is allowed to go barefoot, it actually helps to strengthen the hoof. At least 2 to 3 months of the year the horse should be left without shoes. If nothing else, when the horse will not be used extensively for at least a month, pull the shoes and trim the hoof.

While the hoof is barefoot, attention needs to be given to the condition of the hoof. Every 2 weeks or so the rasp should be taken to the hoof wall to keep it rounded and shaped.

The advantages in proper and frequent hoof trimming are numerous. The horse owner can give appropriate and immediate attention to any problems. If a crack or split is developing, prompt attention can prevent any damage. It is better to trim frequently if only with the rasp than to wait too long and have a problem occur because of an excessively long hoof. Think of the horse's hoof in terms of your finger nails. What happens when nails get long and break off? With young colts, frequent and proper trimming can prevent some conformation faults from occurring and minimize others.

The horse should also be trimmed to go barefoot anytime shoes are removed and are not being put back on immediately. When winter comes and the horse is not to be used for a while or anytime the horse is not to be ridden or used for a month or more, the shoes should be pulled and the horse allowed to go barefoot. This practice will provide for a much healthier foot that will be disease resistant, more resistant to wear and also hold a shoe on better when shoeing is necessary.

Removing the shoe

The first step in trimming or shoeing a horse is to remove the old shoes (if they are still on). Proper removal of the shoes is important because it determines the condition the foot is left in after the removal. If the clinches are not loosened properly, chunks of the hoof can be pulled off with the shoe, leaving rough spots and gaps in the hoof wall. The clinch cutters work very well in preventing this by loosening the clinches so the shoe will come off easily.

Step 1   Bring the foot into the basic position as described and shown in the Hoof Handling section (fig. 18, page 22).

Step 2   If the shoe is to be reused mark the shoe so that it can be put back on the proper foot. Suggestions for marking the shoe are as follows. Take the blade of the clinch cutters and place it on the shoe. Strike it with the hammer to leave a mark on the outside branch of the shoe as you are looking down on it. Strike it near the toe area if it is a front foot and near the heel if it is a rear foot. When you go to put the shoe back on a foot, make sure the mark is to the outside of the foot. (Outside here means furthest from the horse.)

Fig 40. Foot in the shoeing position

Fig 41. Mark the shoe

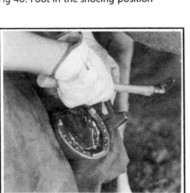

Fig 42. Strike the clinch cutter to loosen the clinch

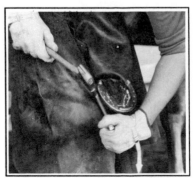

Fig 43. Strike the clinch cutter to loosen the clinch

Step 3   Place the clinch cutter blade under a clinch.

Step 4   Strike the clinch cutter to remove or loosen the clinch. Repeat with all clinches.

Step 5   Place the shoe pull off under the heel area of the shoe on one of the branches of the shoe.

Step 6   Gently push the pull off handle towards the toe. The shoe should loosen some.

Step 7   Place the pull offs under the opposite heel and push towards the toe. *Note: It is important the toe of the foot is supported while the shoe is being loosened. Also it is important that the pull offs are being pushed down toward the toe and not to the side. Damage could result to the pastern area if side pressure is too great.*

Step 8   Repeat as necessary, alternating sides until each branch is loose and the shoe comes off.

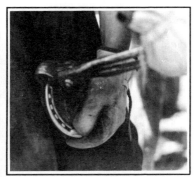

Fig 44. Place pull offs under the heel of the shoe

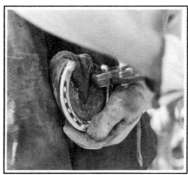

Fig 45. Support the toe as you push the pull offs towards the toe

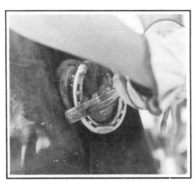

Fig 46. Repeat as necessary alternating sides

Fig 47. Until each branch is loose or the shoe comes off

Trimming

Note-the assumption being made in this section is that the hoof is in overall good condition and has not been neglected or been allowed to have excessive growth. If this is not the case, it is recommended that your farrier be called to trim the hoof and then you can follow up with care in the future. This type of hoof condition that would require the services of your farrier is typical when the horse has not been used for several months or left to run in the back 40 for the winter. The horse owner will receive maximum benefit from doing their own hoof care when the hoof is taken care of on a regular basis.

Step 1   Look at the horse's foot on a flat, level surface. Decide before beginning what needs to be done to balance the foot. Does the foot point to one side or the other? If so then the side it is pointing towards will need a little more hoof wall taken off. If the toes are pointing in then the inside hoof wall should be trimmed (no more than 1/8" lower than the other side). An imaginary line drawn through the center of the pastern should approximate the angle through the hoof.

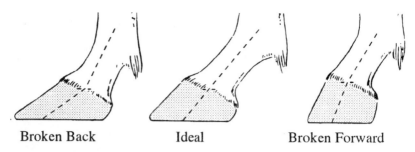

Broken Back   Ideal   Broken Forward

Pastern angle through the hoof
Diagram 4

Under normal circumstances the toe will need to be cut more than the heels. This is because the hoof at the toe grows faster than the hoof at the heel. The most common mistake made is to cut too much heel off when trimming. This causes the angle through the pastern and foot to be too acute and puts extreme pressure on the flexor tendons. For the purpose of horse owners doing their own horses, it is recommended to nipper only the toe area above the A-B line. The A-B line is the imaginary line running perpendicular across the hoof dividing the hoof area into top and bottom halves (see diagram 1, page 10) If any hoof needs to be removed from the heels, use the fine side of the rasp to level them.

Fig 48. Look at the foot (before)

Fig 49. Check angle through pastern and hoof (before)

Fig 50. Look at foot (after)

Fig 51. Check angle (after)

Step 2   Using the hoof knife trim away the "dead" sole. The knife must be held in the palm of the hand so that the sharp edge is facing you. This position may appear to be backwards, but this is the way the knife is designed to be used. Use the curved point of the hoof knife to do the trimming. The dead sole is dull and flaky as opposed to the live sole which is shiny and smooth. Trim the sole only until the composition of the sole changes from dull to shiny. If the area begins to look pink or red, stop trimming immediately, you have gone too far! You need to only trim the sole around the toe area within 1/4" of the white line. The only reason for trimming the sole in a normal, healthy hoof is to find out how far to trim back the excess hoof wall. The rest of the dead sole on the bottom of the foot should be left to wear away naturally and serve as protection for the foot. When trimming to go barefoot, only cut away enough sole to provide a groove to help guide the nippers when cutting. Remember more hoof wall and sole needs to be left on when trimming the hoof to go barefoot.

Fig 52. Trim away the dead sole. Note the proper way to hold the knife

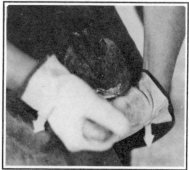

Fig 53. Trim within 1/4" of the white line

Step 3 Trim any excess hoof growth at the bars back to the level of the sole. This is done to prevent them from growing too long, forming a false sole by growing over the bottom of the hoof, or from breaking off and possibly causing lameness.

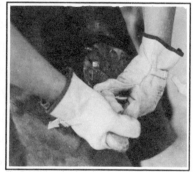

Fig 54. Trim the bar back to the level of the sole

Fig 55. Trim the bar back to the level of the sole

Step 4 Pare away only any ragged or diseased part of the frog. Other than that, leave the frog alone. It serves a very important function (see Anatomy section).

Step 5 Insert the hoof nippers at the toe to the level of the knife groove. Be sure the nippers are cutting perpendicular to the bearing surface of the hoof. That is, the handle of the hoof nippers should rise at a 90 degree angle to the plane of the hoof.

Beginning at the center of the toe, overlap each nipper cut approximately one-half of the nipper edge. Gradually bring each cut up towards the heel so that by the time the quarters are reached the nipper cuts are through the excess hoof wall.

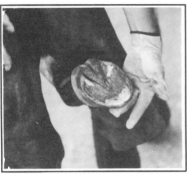
Fig 56. Foot ready for nipper cut

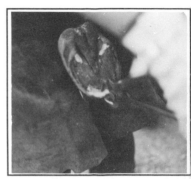
Fig 57. Insert nipper at the toe - overlap each cut

Fig 58. Rasp with long. even strokes

Fig 59. Rasp with long, even strokes

Step 6   Take the rasp to trim the quarters and heel area. Use the fine side of the rasp on the quarters since they are extremely soft and it is very easy to take off too much and make a serious mistake. The sole is lower at the quarters (remember the concave shape of the sole) making the hoof wall appear higher at the quarters then they actually are. Be very careful not to cut the wall low at the quarters. This is the reason only the rasp should be used at this section by beginners.

Rasp only one side at a time and avoid "bouncing" the rasp on the near or close side. Rasp from heel to toe in long even strokes. Only rasp the high spots and continually check to see if it is level and balanced. If a mistake is made and part of the hoof is too low, don't compound the problem by continuing to rasp around it. Learn from the mistake and try to do better next time.

Fig 60. Rasp one side at a time

Fig 61. Avoid "bouncing" the rasp on the near side

Step 7   Take the nippers and using the imaginary A-B line as a guide, nipper the outside hoof wall edge at a 45 degree angle above the A-B line. Take off approximately one half the width of the hoof wall with the nippers. This step will help the beginner determine how much of the foot is to be rasped while rounding the edges.

Fig 62. Nipper the hoof wall edge at a 45 degree angle

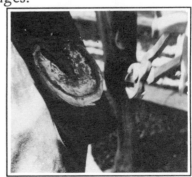

Fig 63. Nipper approximately 1/2 the width of the hoof wall

Fig 64. Nipper around the toe

Fig 65. Put the foot on the stand

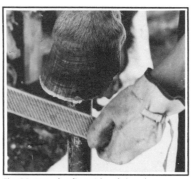
Fig 66. Use the fine side of the rasp

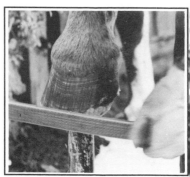
Fig 67. Round the edges of the hoof wall back to the heels

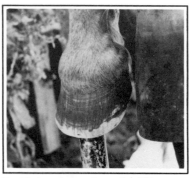
Fig 68. Any obvious flares should be taken off

Fig 69. Blend the flares into the natural angle of the hoof wall

Step 8   Bring the foot up and put it on a foot stand. Take the rasp and round the edges left from the 45 degree nipper cut. This is to keep the hoof from chipping while the horse is barefoot. Continue to round the hoof wall back to the heels. Remember, what you are trying to do is create a 'shoe' for the bottom of the hoof out of the excess hoof wall around the outside of the ground surface of the foot.

Step 9   The foot should also be balanced and any obvious flaring taken off. When rasping flares it is important to not just chop the flare off at a 90 degree angle. Blend the flares into the natural angle of the hoof wall. Keep in mind the natural appearance of a compact healthy hoof.

HOW TO SELECT AND EVALUATE A FARRIER

Even if you will do the majority of hoof care after reading this book, there are still times when you will want a professional farrier to work with you and your horse. I suggest that you have a professional farrier work with your horse at least once a year. This will insure that the feet are healthy and being trimmed and shod properly. It will also give you a chance to work with and learn from a professional.

Here are some suggestions for finding a competent farrier:

1) Contact the American Farriers Association or the Brotherhood of Working Farriers Association. They will be able to send you a list of certified farriers serving your area.

American Farrier's Association
4059 Iron Works Pike
Lexington, KY 40511
Ph: 606-233-7411
Fax: 606-231-7862

Brotherhood of Working Farrier's Association
14013 E. Hwy 136
LaFayette, GA 30728
Ph: 706-397-8047
Fax: 706-397-8047

2) Ask horse owners for the names of farriers they have used whose work was satisfactory.

3) Ask your veterinarian for referrals.

4) Check the classified ads in newspapers or phone books.

5) Check bulletin boards at farm and feed stores.

Once you have some names to call there are some questions and suggestions to help you find a quality professional farrier to work on your horse.

1) Is the farrier on time?

2) Does the farrier take time to question you about your horse before work begins? Questions like:

   a) What is your intended use for the horse in the near future?

   b) Does the horse have any old injuries that might effect the use or restrict movement?

   c) Does the horse have any medical history that effects the way the horse moves (travel or gait faults)?

3) Does the farrier take the time to observe the horse in motion? (Even if the farrier has worked on the horse before, changes in hoof growth or use can effect the horse and hoof care needs).

4) Does the farrier keep a record on the horse showing things like shoe size, date of service and any special requirements? (It is virtually impossible to remember all horses a farrier works with. Keeping complete records will allow the farrier to provide consistent and appropriate service).

Observe the farrier while working with the horse. Does the farrier follow the basic principles of horseshoeing? The steps or the order in which they are done may vary. Everybody does it a little different. But the basic principles should not vary. If something is being done you don't understand, ask why. No competent farrier should mind being asked why a certain procedure is being done. Be wary of the farrier who doesn't want you around while work is being done on your horse. There may be a reason to hide!

It is recommended that no work is done on your horse if you are not around to watch. Besides, watching others will help you learn more about hoof care.

Some additional questions:

1) What are the rates charged for services?

2) What training does the farrier have? (I recommend a graduate of an accredited shoeing school.)

3) Is the farrier capable of corrective shoeing? Even if you do not need corrective shoeing, a farrier that is capable of this will generally have more training and experience. Is the farrier fully equipped for corrective shoeing if necessary—forge, acrylics, pads, etc.? Beware of the farrier that claims to be capable of corrective shoeing but shows up without the required and necessary equipment.

4) Is the farrier a full time farrier?

Note: I strongly feel that in order to do a professional job, to keep up with advances and to be equipped adequately for most situations, your farrier should be a full-time farrier. Besides, if you need something done in an emergency, the chances are better that a full-time farrier would be available rather than trying to schedule around another job.

5) How much lead time is needed to set up an appointment?

6) How are emergency calls handled?

7) Is the farrier familiar with your particular type of horse breed and particular use (hunter, jumper, pleasure, work, etc.)?

Now that you have found a farrier that is qualified and you feel confident with, how do you keep this farrier? Good professional farriers are in demand and they can and do choose horses and owners much as you choose them.

1) Is your horse unruly or hard to handle while working with the hooves? If so expect to pay more for the service and be willing to spend more time and/or money to train the horse to stand for hoof care.

2) Are you available during the time the farrier is scheduled to come? You or someone the horse knows should be available to hold the horse.

3) Is the horse caught and tied in a safe place to work? Do not expect the farrier to chase and catch your horse unless you are willing to pay for this service. Farriers have many appointments and need to keep on schedule to provide professional service to other customers.

4) Do you pay on time for services provided and are you willing to pay a fair price? Most farriers expect to be paid at the time services are provided. If a payment schedule is negotiated, keep to it.

5) Do you provide a safe and secure place to work on the horse? Is the area covered from inclement weather or provides shade when it is hot?

6) Do you cancel appointments?

7) Do you put off needed services until the last minute and then call and expect the farrier to show up at your convenience? A regular scheduled time made in advance will provide the best service for you.

8) Do you follow the suggestions made by the farrier for interim hoof care?

The relationship between you and your farrier is beneficial to both and the responsibility of both. When both you and the farrier recognize each others' responsibilities, then the best service will be provided to your horse.

Evaluating a Farrier's Shoeing Job

General Impression

Do the feet look better than when the job was started?

Is the horse in any obvious pain, does it limp or appear lame when walked?

Does the foot look balanced and shaped and does the shoe look like it fits the balanced and shaped foot?

Preparation of the Hoof

Was the frog trimmed only enough to remove rough edges and left large enough to make contact with the ground?

Was only dead sole removed and was excessive paring of sole avoided?

Was the hoof shaped, was the angle through the pastern carried into the angle of the hoof and was the hoof surface left level?

Were each pair of feet left the same size (front and hind) as well as the same length (between toe and heel)?

Fit of Shoe

Does the shoe fit? Is the shoe the right size to cover the buttress area of the heel? Does the shoe fit the outer edge of the hoof and is there area left for expansion of the heel from the last nail hole back?

Is the shoe the proper style and weight for the intended use of the horse?

Was the shoe properly leveled? Are there any noticeable gaps between the hoof wall and the shoe?

Was there any rasping of the foot after the shoe was fitted and nailed? Was the hoof radically rasped at an unnaturally looking angle creating a "dubbed" look to the foot?

Clinching and Nailing

Are the nails driven at the proper height? Are the nails driven to a consistent height with other nails in the hoof?

Were the nails used the smallest size that was practical for the size of the shoe? Were Regular head nails used for a reset job?

Are the clinches properly seated into the hoof wall and left smooth to the touch?

Now that you have had an opportunity to try working on your own horses' hooves, you may be interested in the companion book to *Hooftrimming for Horseowners*. If you feel comfortable trimming your horse and wish to explore and learn about shoeing, *Horseshoeing for Horseowners* is written by the same author and follows the same step-by-step format to guide you through the basic methods of shoeing, nailing, clinching, selecting shoes and tools.

H.F.H. Publications
P.O. Box 300
Lenoxdale, MA 01242
1-800-247-6551

What I have tried to do in the preceding pages is to bring basic knowledge to you — the horse owner — about daily hoof care, hooftrimming and horseshoeing. I realize — and hope that you do too — that working with horses' hooves is a lifelong learning experience. All that can be presented in this book is a base, a starting point for further learning. Read the book over and over until you understand the principles involved, then go to your horse and walk through the steps. Visualize what should be done and then try it. Take the book with you to the horse. Use it while you are with the horse. Whenever you have a farrier work with your horse, watch what your farrier does and ask questions. Learn from this book and from others.

Above all, Good Luck! I hope you enjoy working with horses as much as I have.

(signature)

— —

Please send me _____ copies of *Horseshoeing for Horseowners* at $20.00 ($17.95 plus $2.05 shipping & handling) for each book to:

NAME _____

ADDRESS _____

CITY, STATE, ZIP _____

MasterCard ☐   VISA ☐

Call 1-800-247-6551
or mail this card to HFH Publications

CARD NO: ⬚⬚⬚⬚ ⬚⬚⬚⬚ ⬚⬚⬚⬚ ⬚⬚⬚⬚⬚

EXP. DATE: _____

SIGNATURE _____